SEEING IN THE SPIRIT MY TESTIMONY

David Hess

Introduction

This is my testimony. We overcome by the blood of the Lamb and word of our testimony according to Revelations. I have seen in the spirit realm since I was a child. Many people seem to want to, but I don't think many could really handle it very well. This is simply my account to share what I have seen to stir up faith and encourage you to share your testimony and faith how The LORD has touched you or used you or even someone else in something spectacular or even seemingly ordinary although with God nothing is just simply ordinary even when we think it is. I pray your perspective and view of the unseen to be expanded and maybe even challenged. This is not to replace anything in the way of scripture. I pray that it does nothing but confirm the scriptures and give all glory to God our Father and Lord Jesus Christ and the giver of all spiritual gifts as He wills the Spirit of the Holy One.

In this time of growing darkness may we be reminded that we serve the LORD of Hosts. There are more with us than there are with them. The reason we have any accounts of spiritual things such as angels and demons and all the other visions described by Old and New Testament servants is the ministry of seers. Not all prophets are seers, but all seers seem to be prophets and see with the gift of discerning of spirits. It seemed good to make the format of this book more of just sharing my story verses making it another teaching book, but I do pray you learn something from this and if you walk in these gifts may it bring you encouragement, that you are not alone.

Dedications

I dedicate this book to my parents, Gary and Thelma Hess who have always encouraged me in my giftings and callings and did their best to raise me in the ways of The LORD so that when I got old, I would not depart from them even though for a brief time I tried.

Especially my dad who I believe helped me pick up some writing skills and who walks now with the angels and our LORD Jesus, until we can all walk together again. I love you and miss you very much.

Thank You. Blessings.

TABLE OF CONTENTS

CHAPTER 1
The Beginning: a Good Place to Start.

I am a preacher's kid. I am called to ministry as well, but just so you know. I was one of those ankle biters who was either in children's church or playing or sleeping under the pew. I am shy by nature. I can certainly voice my opinion but with those I feel more comfortable with unless the anointing comes on and then watch out. I am saying I consider myself a normal guy. I am not overly spiritual or more holy than anyone. I do strive to be spiritually mature and walk in holiness out of love, faith and a motive to please our heavenly Father and Lord Jesus Christ.

My family is from Iowa but when I was two years old, we moved to Oklahoma, so my dad, Bro. Gary Hess, could go to a bible school, Rhema Bible Training Center. When I was five, we moved to Kentucky to help a couple that my parents met in

Oklahoma and start a church in Frankfort. My dad was able to get a job with the Department of Education. Eventually, my parents would start Circle of Love Ministries and started an itinerant traveling ministry throughout the states that make up the Ohio Valley. We went to many different meetings and I sat under many other preachers as well.

I believe that I was seven and we were at a meeting. There was another minister preaching. He was a prophet named Oliver. I remember being in the front pew with my mom. It was a small country church. Stage in the front and exit door in the back. I don't remember what he was preaching about and I can't even tell you his name right now. In the middle of his preaching, though, it seemed out of the blue, he pointed to the back and said, "I see an angel over that exit sign". I looked back and I didn't see anything but he made God so real to me. I prayed right there and then that I would be able to minister in a similar fashion when I grew up. I wanted so much to make God real to others and this guy had made Him to me at that moment.

Scripture, at the end of the day, is the final authority but when we as believers can share our testimonies and supernatural things we may have encountered or experienced, hopefully, it will help build another's faith. What he saw inspired that prayer and little did I know how soon that prayer would be answered.

The Tall Man Outside Our Door

As I had said, our family had moved to Kentucky. My parents initially were helping a couple start a church and then went into traveling ministry themselves. We had moved into a house in Frankfort, Ky. If anyone knows Frankfort, it is built in and around a valley and there are many areas and subdivisions that are hilly. The house we lived in was built on a hill. The main level and front door went out to the top side of the hill and then the back was the kitchen area. The back door went out of the kitchen onto a balcony with stairs that led down to the garage, driveway and second level. You had to walk up essentially two stories to get up to our kitchen door or stand on the balcony.

Shortly after the meeting with that prophet, my mom, brother and I were eating in the kitchen. I can't remember if it was breakfast or lunch. Mom was washing some dishes and I was at the kitchen table facing pretty much our kitchen door. All of a sudden, I saw what appeared to be a man but he was so tall he essentially had to bend down to look through the door window. I believe he smiled. I ran thinking, who is this tall man standing outside our window who doesn't look quite like a man but he is definitely on our balcony and surely had to walk up the stairs. I ran to the door and opened it and no one was there. I looked up at the sky and it was a scene where sunrays were coming through the clouds. I believe I had just witnessed an angel on our balcony looking through our window, smiling.

I tried to explain to mom what I had seen and she believed I had too. I told her then about my prayer and if I had perhaps done something wrong to ask to see angels. She was so gracious to encourage me. She explained then, as I will give the same advice to others who desire to see in the spirt, it is unwise to seek things out unless you are prepared. There are other things in the spirit realm other than just angels. Many people have been misled by visions of "angels" We must weigh all experience by the infallible Word of God, the scriptures. Yet my prayer was said in innocence and a desire to bring glory to God, not myself and the gifts and callings of God are without repentance and can be revealed at an early age.

I am hearing more and more young children having open visions, seeing angels and having spiritual dreams. These gifts should be cultivated, not despised. A young mind is easier to teach and raise versus an older one, even though we can all respond to the callings of The LORD at different times in our life. Moses was called to be the deliverer since he was sent down the river in the basket but did not comprehend his calling till he was in the wilderness as a stuttering old shepherd. We are not sure the exact age Jesus knew He was the Anointed One of Israel and savior of the world but we know from scripture He knew His true Father at least by twelve and was wise in the scriptures well beyond his youth and family's station. I say that since He baffled even the learned at the temple. Jesus was not raised by a rabbi but by a carpenter. The Holy Spirit was His teacher. But I am certain even Mary and Joseph did all they could to raise Him as they knew.

We need to do all we can to cultivate the callings of our children and teach them scriptures no matter how much we think they understand or not. But most of all introduce them to Jesus. Teach them about the Teacher, the Spirit of the Holy One. Let us not despise youth or age or gifts but learn to walk in humility in all things unto the glory of our Father.

First Engagements

It was not long after the experience in the kitchen that I would see my first engagement of angels and demons and how they can interact with services in a church. My parents were having a meeting at a church in southern Kentucky. I was around eight at this time. My dad would be preaching this Sunday morning. My parents, brother and I are in the front. It was during worship and although I don't know any of the circumstances that were happening within the church I could just tell there was some kind of darkness over the church. The people just didn't look happy, and well, you would hope that if you are in the House of the LORD, you would be more happy.

At some point during worship, I was allowed to see in the spirit. I saw demons all over the stage. I was pretty young, so I didn't really have any chance to be indoctrinated in any way about demons. I did think it strange that all these demons would just be roaming around the church but it would explain the atmosphere that I was feeling.

Demons are nothing to fear. They are fallen ones. Their lot is with the god of this world from the anointed cherub that was tasked with the guardianship of the earth from the beginning. He transgressed in heaven with his pride and thought he could ascend above the Most High.

These demons were of different shapes and sizes. Spirits, whether demons, angels or the Spirit of God, are not confined in one form as physical bodies. There was one that took the form of a dark, condensed cloud with many red eyes. He seemed like a leader. One looked like a griffin from mythology, half lion and half eagle. It makes you wonder if the myths and legends of gods and monsters from the eons were inspired by demons whether by thought imagination or someone saw something in the spirit. The enemy does have a level of power. We should not be ignorant of it. He also draws power from mankind especially through fear. But greater is He in us than he that is in the world.

I tried to tell my dad but he initially thought I was playing around. Thankfully, my mom sensed that they should listen to what I was saying. I told them what I saw then they asked me what we should do. At first I thought you're the parents and preachers you should know!! What came to my heart though was the scripture *"he inhabits the praises of his people"* Ps. 22:3

So I told them that we need to encourage the people to really enter into praise and worship. That they cannot go through the motions but that their faith in The LORD must arise to enter into his courts and see God's presence manifest. Light and darkness cannot dwell together. I was still too shy to share myself, so dad shared what I had seen and encouraged all of us to enter into God's presence with worship in spirit and truth. Then I saw a haze come into the room and up toward the ceiling, I saw angels standing in orderly rows.

It was almost like a choir or a host of angels standing at attention. They had brass skin, glowing blondish hair, white robes and just hovering. They were around 7-8 feet tall with no wings. Some angels have wings like cherubim and seraphim we read from the scripture but these did not. They were singing with us. As much as I thought maybe they would engage with the demons and fight them.

It seemed more effective for them to sing with us. I am sure that they would have fought if such inspired prayers were commanded for their aid but the saints and angels singing the praises of the Almighty brought His presence and glory into that place and as the demons were still flying around chaotically, they seemed like they were choking. Soon thereafter, they seemed to vanish. They either left or my eyes were kept from seeing them.

The pastor was sitting on the stage, stooped down and seemed to be praying. If you have seen the thinking man staturue he was kind of in that posture. A large angel came up behind him and put a blanket on him that said "peace" on it. It was truly a sight to behold. I want to say my dad preached but I don't remember much after that. That scene is burned into my memory and even though I may forget many other things throughout my life and as I get older but those kind of experiences have never left me.

If you have a desire to see in the spirit, pray very carefully. There is a price to pay and a responsibility to bear. You can open yourself up to darkness, witchcraft and demonic activity. You need much wisdom. At the same time, I am hearing more and more of children seeing in the spirit and seeing angels and so if it does seem your calling or the calling of someone you know, I would just encourage a great walk with the LORD. A strong prayer life and faithful to the study of the Word of God.

These are the beginnings of my testimony and journey with The LORD, the supernatural and spirit realm. I pray that in some way it blesses you and makes God real to you. May it stir your faith and if you don't know Jesus Christ as your savior, you can ask him into your life and He will change you forever.

CHAPTER 2
Fear Not

It has been said that the scriptures say fear not or don't be afraid around 365 times. A time for each day of the year. The reverential fear of the LORD is one thing but perfect love casts out all sense of terror and dread. We are not to be subject to fear. The Enemy and demons feed on it like sugar. The Enemy is crafty as he has always been since the garden. He will remind us of our past tempt us unto sin and then make us feel guilty for falling into sin. He will corrupt and distort the truth. He is the father of lies and a murderer from the beginning.

In the 7th century Pope Boniface IV had set All Saints day for the Catholic Church originally on May 13th but apparently in the next century the Church would transfer it to November 1st to "Christianize" pagan holidays perhaps celebrated at that time celebrated especially in Europe as the Holy Roman Empire and the Church was strengthening its political stance among those that still worshipped 'old gods.' Perhaps there were good intentions initially but now the day that would be a holy eve since Nov. 1st was to be a holy day is now Halloween. A day in the world and church we celebrate death and fear. Things that the Body of the Messiah should have no part in.

Why am I bringing this up? I have seen first hand how fear plays a part in the power given to the Enemy and the fallen. I personally can't watch horror movies. There are too many things inspired by hell in horror movies that I just can't watch. Not all movies are demonic but certainly some are. Some creatures in movies are inspired and remind me of things I've seen and others just have an attitude or presence about them and you are allowing that dark presence into your house and then justify it by saying "it's not real."

Some of you might be familiar with the Walking Dead. It was very popular a few years ago and I can't watch it or a lot of other zombie movies because they look like demons or at least some of them. The sound they make remind me of demons as well. I can't watch it. Freddie Kreuger also reminds of demons I've seen.

We must be careful what we celebrate. Even ex-witches and Satanist will tell you that Christians should not celebrate Halloween. Even if its just about fun and candy to you a poisoned apple is still poisoned. At the time of this writing in 2023 we are still getting over ever so slowly the cov-id 19 pandemic. So much I believe in 2020 of what was reported gave people hysteria. When we look at the real numbers reported after the fact we see that the impact of fatality was not much different then the regular flu or some of the other corona viruses such as H1-N1 or swine flu. All the deaths and loss is nothing to snuff at. But this plague definitely had some demonic influence on it. I personally believe Satan himself had his hand on this. The contributing factor to have such a strong demonic association with this plague is fear. Our fear gave it power.

I say all this to set the stage for my next encounter which would be a few years later after my first. As I said earlier my parents started to travel and preaching especially on prayer in the Kentucky and the Ohio Valley. In 1990 The LORD had sent dad on his first mission trip to England and expanding the vision and assignment of Circle of Love Ministries to nations that had been part of the British Empire back in the day. The first nation outside the U.S. The LORD gave was Britain. In 1992 we moved to England to the county of Kent in the town of Ramsgate off the coast of the English Channel. We lived there for a year and it was one of the fondest years of my life. We had connected with a church there in Ramsgate. The church had rented out an old theater for it's services. Halloween is very big in England. It is mainly a protestant nation but it also has people that remember the pagan ways of the Isle. These attitudes from the church and from the world only lift up the devil.

It was Halloween and the church we connected with was having a church service to celebrate God instead of Halloween. During worship I saw creatures that reminded me of zombies or Freddie Krueger and some other creatures of horror. I was twelve years old now. I wasn't as shy to speak especially since I knew most people there and many of them were of our youth group. So I asked to share what I was seeing and just encouraged us to really worship in Spirit and Truth. The devil is real but God is even more so. He is greater. He inhabits the praises of His people.

When we really entered in I saw similarly angels showed up. They did not fight but just sang with us. They were standing in the middle of the theater chairs like the chairs weren't even there. They looked ready to fight but they simply sang with us. As I felt the presence of God coming into the theater those demons looked like they were choking or in pain. It reminded me of the story of the demon possessed man who had many demons in him and Yeshua (Jesus) demanded the name of the demon(s) They told Yeshua their name was Legion (for we are many).

They asked Yeshua if He had come to torture them before the time of their appointed punishment.

Matt. 8-28-34.

Demons cannot stand the Presence of the Almighty. We must live lives of worship and that does not mean just songs but in how we live and speak and treat one another. May we all live lives full of faith, full of the Spirit, full of prayer and praise. May we live lives with courage, boldness and without fear!

You adulteresses [disloyal sinners-flirting with the world and breaking your vow to God]! Do you not know that being the world's friend [that is, loving the things of the world] is being God's enemy? So whosoever chooses to be a friend of the world makes himself an enemy of God. Or do you think that the scripture says to no purpose that the [human] spirit which He has made to dwell in us lusts with envy? But He gives us more and more grace [through the power of the Holy Spirit to defy sin and live an obedient life that reflects both our faith and gratitude for our salvation]. Therefore, it says, " GOD IS OPPOSED TO THE PROUD AND HAUGHTY, BUT [continually] GIVES [the gift of] GRACE TO THE HUMBLE [who turn away from self-righteousness]."

So Submit to [the authority of] God. Resist the devil [stand firm against him]and he will flee from you.

James 4:4-7 Amp.

CHAPTER 3
Angel Worship, Heavenly Robots, Fellow Servants.

What a title. There is a great spectrum of beliefs that tend to not have their roots in scripture. I had many more experiences than what I described thus far. I am just now getting to the place where I am publicly sharing these things. I would not share if I thought for one moment that these testimonies somehow took away from Jesus and the Glory and Worship that belongs to God alone. That is certainly not my intention.

After High School and having a year where I was mad at God and did not want to go into ministry, I finally got over my rebellious year and decided I needed to go to bible school. I attended Rhema Bible Training Center from 1999-2002. I went 3 years. I learned many things about ministry and other great truths about scripture. One of the greatest gifts that Rhema gave me was learning Hermeneutics, how to study the scriptures to be able divide, discern and interpret scripture unto the whole counsel and wisdom of God.

It is not like I was ignorant of the bible or scripture. I had been raised in a minister's home. I had experienced things I could not explain but neither could others to the point that I could say yes this happened in the bible too. I will be forever grateful for the ministry of Kenneth E. Hagin. A father of the faith to many including myself. I am grateful to have been taught under him directly just before his passing in 2003. I was even honored to be part of his funeral service. His teachings about the prophetic ministry and his own experiences helped me so much to feel like I wasn't alone. The devil will do everything he can to talk you out of your calling and gifting. Do not let him.

I say all that to say is that at some point in studying scripture to better understand my own experiences I came across this verse and many others have used this verse negatively to discourage sharing of one's supernatural experience and used to say that if you share visions that you are being unscriptural. It was this scripture.

"Let no one keep defrauding you of your prize by delighting in self-abasement and the worship of the angels, taking his stand on visions he has seen, inflated without cause by his fleshly mind, and not holding fast to the head, from whom the entire body, being supplied and held together by the joints and ligaments, grows with a growth which is from God." Col. 2:18,19 NAS

After reading that scripture I became very discouraged in sharing publicly many of the visions I had seen. The last thing I would do would be to condone angel worship or try to toot my own horn because of a vision. Yet I struggled since this was my prayer from a child not to exalt angels or myself but to help people realize how real God was. It has been only in the past recent years that I came to better understand the context of why Paul said this to the Colossians. It is good to understand that this letter of Paul was written to a new church in the city of Colossae in now modern Turkey. We don't have scripture to confirm he actually visited them; but only heard about them. It was a thriving city at one point a "great city" as one historian put it. By Paul's day, it had dwindled some and being still a town of commerce Jews traveled and moved to all parts of the then Roman empire. We see that very well in Acts 2 when so many came from all different nations back to the Temple to celebrate Shavuot/Feast of Weeks.

Some where along the way either by Jewish influence or others adopted into angel worship. Michael is attributed to opening up a spring for the city. There was an angel cult. Funny enough or maybe not so funny the Catholic church opened up the Church of St. Michael in the city of Colossae in the 8th century. Apparently, we can deduce, from Paul's writings people used visions they had to give themselves prominence and this was only exacerbated by angel worship.

I can tell you that as majestic and tall and marvelous the angels I have seen are they don't compare to our God. We are made just a little lower than the angels the Psalms declare so how great can they be compared to the absolute Glory and Majesty of the LORD of Hosts, so heaven bows down and sing worthy and the

Seraphim and elders and creatures around the throne declare Holy Holy Holy is the LORD Almighy as Revelation visualizes this majestic scene around the throne that all the angels worship The Almighty alone.

I have also heard people talk about angels as if they are just robots. I heard a sermon once that described angels as robots of heaven. They serve us and will do our bidding which in a way is true but really the idea of angels and "robots" is ludicrous. Angels have their own will. Satan and the fallen ones that followed him according to Revelation 12 or the angels that left their original order to come down to earth and have relations with women that would produce the Nephalim according to Genesis 6. Angels have their own wills. Thankfully those that kept their loyalty and righteousness are more than those against us forever damned with Satan having no plan of redemption as humanity does. Perhaps that is where their hate comes from. Jesus did not take on the form of angels to redeem them. It is only humanity that salvation has been made. HalleluYah!

The best approach when thinking about angels is understanding they are our fellow servants. Listen to what John says in Revelation.

"I, John am the one who heard and saw these things. And when I heard and saw, I fell down to worship at the feet of the angel who showed me these things. But he said to me, "Do not do that. I am a fellow servant of yours and of your brethren the prophets and of those who heed the words of this book. Worship God." Rev. 22:8,9

They are our fellow servants and they also minister to us and for us our behalf as we are heirs of salvation according to Hebrews 1:14. Humanity and angels are called to worship and serve God together. He is the

LORD of Hosts in heaven and in the earth and we as believers have access in the Name of Jesus to have them do the business of the kingdom of Heaven in the earth in the spirit realm. I will not go into all the scriptures here, but I do recommend reading Hebrews Chapters 1 and 2 that go into much more detail and depth.

Lastly, we must understand angels are a different creature all together from humans. When we pass on and take on our heavenly bodies which are different then our glorified bodies we will take in the Age to Come, we don't become angels. As much as I enjoy "It's a Wonderful Life" none of us are like Clarence and earn our wings. Not all angles have wings that I have seen. Cherubim usually have two and Seraphim are described with six wings but to my knowledge according to experience and scripture none of humanity become an angel to earn their wings. They were already created at some point before or after the creation of Earth. We see this evident with Satan and the Cherubim that stood guard at the garden after Adam's and Eve's fall. None of humanity would enter heaven at least till Enoch.

So now that I hope you understand the intent of this book that we should not be given over to angel worship or use our visions for personal gain but at the same time the scriptures are full of testimonies of visions and many of them being from prophets and seers and one of the ministries of the prophet is to see into the spirit and discern what is going on. So, I do not boast in what I have seen. All that I have experienced has been to the will and grace of the Holy Spirit for all spiritual gifts are to His will. All we can do is yield and follow his leading and stay humble when He is willing to use us to minister to people. May we all remember angles have will and emotions much like us and there are more for us than there are against us. They will minister on our behalf because we are heirs of salvation. We also are fellow servants all called to worship the One who is worthy.

CHAPTER 4
Learning a Thing or Three

During my time at Rhema Bible College I went through a few experiences as well. It helped to be in an environment with like minded believers and fellow students hungry for the things of God. The best thing that Bible College equipped me with was hermeneutics that taught me how to study the Bible for myself and to understand the scriptures in ways I did not growing up. It helped me understand my past experiences and I believe even opened doors for me to experience more.

Initially when I moved to Tulsa, Oklahoma I had the opportunity to live with a couple in a bungalow. I had some wonderful experiences up there. It was secluded and peaceful and I came to understand some things for my own self. I also worked for the ministry that had the Bible college. They had a campus wide project of putting up Christmas lights. We put them up from September to November. We then took them down from January to around March or April. It was during this time of taking classes in the morning and then working in the afternoon all of us on that crew were hungry for the things of God. We were hungry for His Word learning about faith and be excited about the supernatural.

During this time it was pretty common to go to classes during the day work in the afternoon putting up Christmas lights all over campus and then getting off a little early on Wednesday nights to be able to do to mid-week service. I grew up in the Word of Faith/Charismatic movement in the 80's and 90's where the outpouring of the Spirit wasn't uncommon as it seems like today. I believe people expect God to move sovereignly when He wants to but He also wants us to want to. That is why the message of faith and having faith in God and coming to Him and believing that HE IS, is so important. We can certainly get off in our motives and the scriptures in James tell us that if we don't have an answer to our prayers we have not asked and if we say that we have asked but still no answer we have asked with wrong motives. James 4:3

At the time of this writing I know so many have prayed to the end of the 2020/2021 plague to end and seemingly to no avail or no answer in the timeframe we had hoped for. It is only now in 2023 we are seeing a significant drop in cases. Much of that is due to fear and having the wrong motives to get back to our own wickedness. Having Church but having hearts far from Him. Much has to do with allowing to hear the voice of the Enemy and believe a lie rather than hold on to the Truth, disavow the prophets and not understand why things went the way they did these past few years.

Jesus came to seek and save the lost starting with the Jews for the sake of the covenant with Abraham, Moses and David but also to all that would believe and over and over we see how many people received from Jesus their healing and Jesus said to them "your faith has made you whole".

Faith does not control God or even move Him to touch us in a certain way to our own lusts and desires. Faith moves us to Him so that we might touch Him and that is what changes us, heals us and takes us from Glory to Glory. Our faith touching His grace is when the supernatural happens, it is when revival can happen.

Well during one of these midweek services it seemed that it would be just another service or would it. The senior pastor was out of town, one of the associate pastors was going to speak this Wednesday or at least he was scheduled to. The associate pastor was a great teacher but not known in flowing in moves of the spirit as much as others. There was another associate pastor and he was known for that. They called him the wild child. The youngest of the associate pastors at the time and he knew how to flow in the Spirit of the Holy One.

He came up to the pulpit to just give the announcements and at that moment my eyes were opened to see a large Cherub above the stage. He was very large, the largest angel I had seen up to that time. He was at least 15 foot tall and had a 30 foot wingspan. He was the first angel I recall at that point in my life having wings. He held a box in his hand.

The church that was at the Bible College was relatively large. The main auditorium could seat around five thousand people. Above the stage were screens that could face everyone. The auditorium was like a crescent theater. My co-workers, friends and I were sitting somewhat to the side closer to the front. When I saw the Cherub I said within myself "who is that"? A voice so loud and commanding that I was positive that it was external but probably not audible to anyone else but me. The voice said " he is a Cherub sent from the presence of the Most High, come to bring blessing to the people".

As soon as I heard that I was like yes LORD bring the blessing! I prayed that the pastor would catch what the Spirit of God was doing. Well he did the anointing came on him and even though he was supposed to just give the announcements he said that he felt led to lay hands on everyone. The Lord is so amazing. He is the Most High He Is self sufficient. Does He need any of us. Well no He doesn't really 'need' any of us. But then again HE IS love so creation reflects an inert desire for all of us. We are more prone to do what we want than what we need. God did not 'need us' but he does want us. He uses angels and mankind to fulfill His purposes and he uses angels to minister to Himself and us as heirs unto salvation. HE IS YaHaVaH Sabaoth, The LORD of Hosts of heaven and earth.

The giant angel in all his majesty that I beheld was just a dim flicker comapared to our LORD and yet the LORD chose to send the cherub from His presence with blessing of refreshing and his goodness which was imparted by a man through the laying on of hands. The Enemy is doing all he can to deter us from kingdom order and principle. The Enemy is trying to make us afraid and doubtful of one another of getting close to one another and laying hands on each other to impart healing virtue and blessing. Surely the return of Jesus is near and the revealing of the son of perdition that would oppose him is near as well. But it is written that we would be taken away first. If you are reading this then we are still here and until we are raptured away we must resist and restrain till that day.

Well the associate pastor had everyone in that auditorium come up in 3 lines. It was a large front area but even then not all could go up at once. But he laid hands on all of us and then the spirit moved. We sang and danced and others were slain and laughed in the Holy Spirit. It was a glorious time. I was even given some personal direction during that service. I learned that El Elyon desires to use us all that night.

There were other times in the bungalow that The LORD showed me how many angels were assigned to me. There were times that I would wake up and angels were at the foot of my bed. They are not our robots, they are our fellow servants. Different in creation, they are not human but they are probably the only other sentient beings other Satan and demons, in all of creation. I personally think they deserve our respect.

If we are more conscience of their work in our lives, I believe it will go better for us. They worship with us in our services, they protect us and fight the enemy on our behalf, they bring us messages and carry our declarations. They report our dealings to heaven and take account of our good works or disobedience. They look from a distance as we who are spirits encased in dust and ponder the power of salvation.

Elohim did not take on the form of angels to redeem them so there is no salvation for angels only righteousness or damnation but humanity has a chance for change and we must do all we can to share that chance to live that chance out through the Grace and Love of Jesus Christ our LORD.

Seeing Human Spirits

We must be very conscience that we are spirit beings with a soul that consists of mind will and emotions encased in flesh made from dust.

We are what we call a triune being. From the beginning we have been made in the image of Elohim.

Then God said, "Let us make humankind in our image, in the likeness of ourselves; and let them rule over the fish in the sea, the birds in the air, the animals, and over al the earth, and over every crawling creature that crawls on the earth." Gen. 1:26

When we are talking about discernment of spirits in relation to humans (each other) we can get a place in the spirit where we see the human spirit. We can see by this gift if one is born again or not. We can see if our light is dim or bright in accordance with our faith and fire for God. We can see if there are things (demons, unclean spirits) attached to us. I have seen demons on people that were born again (confessed Jesus Christ as their savior) oppressing them. This is different than possession which we will get into more detail later. The gift of discernment when dealing with people should not be confused with picking up an attitude or having a feeling about someone's intentions.

People have been judged poorly in saying that they operate in the gift of discernment and have just simply been making deductive conclusions. That is to not say that people have picked up on people's intentions or attitudes using this method. But we have to see that there is a difference of this which is more of the soul and the supernatural gift of discernment which is a revelation gift.

Discernment of spirits is talking about judging with the eye. To be able to see a spirit, whether it be an angel, demon or human spirit is supernatural. You are seeing into the spirit with your natural eyes supernaturally. One could say as far as visions go it is an open vision. But visions are a different topic we won't go into depth here. In many ways I hope I have stated plainly what discerning of spirits is and is not.

With that said while I was at Rhema Bible College I was living with roommates very fervent for the things of The LORD. We went out to witness many times and sometimes we just drove around Tulsa praying and seeking The LORD, getting deep into the spirit. It was during one of these outings that we were praying that I really got drunk in the spirit and was really into it. If you have never been drunk in the Spirit you may not understand but I encourage you to look into it.

While I was drunk in the Spirit I was starting to see in the spirit realm. This felt like the first time where the curtain of men's spirits were unveiled. My roommates and friends that I was with at the time decided they wanted to go to Wal-Mart. It was late in the evening and well we all know that many characters come out to Wal-Mart at night. At first I didn't want to go in because I felt like the presence of the Spirit was so overwhelming I could hardly walk. With their help we started wandering around trying to be led. I saw people but I also saw them as if I had x-ray vision. I wasn't seeing their muscles, tissues or bones but their spirits. Some of them looked dark with no light. It reminded me of the darkness I have seen demons have. Even though those demons usually took on some kind of form. It was just a darkness with no light. I could tell that the people I saw without any light were not born again. But I could also tell who did have light. Some people's light was much brighter than others. I even saw one person that was working there. He was putting up inventory and he had a light that was very dim but all over his body was demons. He was not possessed but oppressed. They were not in him but around him. The demons took on the form of snakes, spiders and other large bug-like creatures crawling all over him. Are you still ready to see in the spirit realm? Many want to see angels but are you ready to see demons as well.

Interestingly enough, I didn't have an unction to do anything about those demons. He was working right along oblivious to what was around him and yet I knew that even though his light was very dim he had some faith in Christ but there were other beliefs decisions and attitudes that apparently had opened the door to this. Little did I know then that I would end up working with that young man a few months later. We talked about The LORD and I was able to witness to him a bit. I did not see anything when I worked with him. But based on certain lifestyle decisions he talked about I could see why perhaps what opened the door to his oppression. I never cast out anything but I pray that in our conversations he was able to find a greater walk with The LORD.

We can't always tell where people are at just by looking at them in the natural.

We can't tell usually when a person is saved or unsaved. Those with the dim lights were not allowing the Spirit of the Holy One to help them shine and yet Isaiah tells us to Arise and shine for our Light has come. We are the Light in this world. Our Heavenly Father is the Father of Lights. We are those lights and we need to allow our Light from our spirit man to shine as bright as it can. It was a little surprising whose spirits were dark and bright. You could not deduce it from just seeing them in the natural.

Unless the Spirit of the Holy One is opening our eyes supernaturally then we need to see everyone as we take them. Let us not assume they are dark or bright. May we be led and simply share Jesus with our walk with our talk with our Light. We need oil for our lamps to light the fire of the Ruach (the Spirit). You don't know who you work with, what they are going through. Even if they say they believe or go to church we don't always know what a person is going through or what they might be carrying (good and bad). All we can do is make sure that our Light is shining for Jesus and with Jesus and all that we do in our deeds, actions thought and speech glorifies our Father and we can potentially change someone's life and not even know it.

As we get into the next chapter we will see that there are times we will need to directly deal with the devil. It says that those who believe will cast out demons and so if you are a believer that is part of your faith. It is a part of the commission as much as it is to share our faith and lay hands on the sick so they will recover. Mark 16

CHAPTER 5
Into The Darkness

"We pray that you will be continually strengthened with all the power that comes from his glorious might; so that you will be able to persevere and be patient in any situation, joyfully giving thanks to the Father for have you made fit to share in the inheritance of His people in the Light. He has rescued us from the domain of darkness and transferred us into the Kingdom of His dear Son" 1 Col. 1:11-13 CJB

We are no longer in the domain of darkness and it is not my intention to give any credit or spotlight to the Enemy but is good to know who your enemy is and how to deal with him. As we have testified previously I have seen into the spirit realm since seven. I have seen demons since then. I am not afraid of demons. We have no reason to be afraid of them.

There is only one time where I felt so attacked it gave me pause but we will get into that in a little bit.

I wanted to share a few other experiences concerning demons. I believe it is important to have a sound perspective on demons as believers. Yeshua told us not to rejoice that we have authority over them although it is essential in our walk with Christ to know that we do have authority. It is a sign as a believer to cast out devils. Even more important though is to rejoice that our names are written in the Lamb's Book of Life. This tells me that our position in Christ speaks more of our destiny and relation with Christ than sticking it to our enemies who are already damned for their rebellion. We should be settled in our eternal placement and remember their final destination as well.

I have already mentioned seeing demons since I was seven. I have had other experiences that became more direct and personal. Verses took on greater light and meaning in a few different services. Once such experience involved when I first came home to visit after attending Bible College my first semester. My parents had moved to another house while being at Rhema in Oklahoma. The house they moved into while I was away seemed nice enough. My parents conveyed that since they had moved in that some weird supernatural things were happening. Things turning on by themselves or other things one might associate with a haunting if you were to believe such things.

To make things abundantly clear I do not believe in human ghosts that stay after passing and haunt places. It is unscriptural. There are familiar spirits and unclean spirits that the god of this world allows to roam the earth. They seem to take on the form of people that have passed. Human spirits are not stuck here. If anything those who practice witchcraft and worship Satan might call up a soul from hell for deceptive purposes. We see this with the witch of Endor and Saul calling up the spirit of Samuel under Old Covenant. 1 Sam. 28.

No soul or person that had passed went to heaven under Old Covenant. The only two exceptions of people who went to Heaven because they did not die were Enoch and Elijah. Since there is a time for all to die, it is likely that at some point they will be sent as the two witnesses described in Revelation. As for believers in Christ under the new and everlasting covenant of the Last Adam and Lamb of YWHW, if we have passed from our bodies then we will be with The LORD in heaven. The Enemy nor any other person can call up a human spirit who is now among the witnesses of The Presence of He who was dead but now is alive forevermore. The Amen and Faithful

Witness is now their home. We will see our loved ones.

At the time of this writing, my dad Rev. Gary Hess went to be with The LORD two years ago. We will see him and all those that have accepted Yeshua as Messiah. His return is imminent and the days are evil, men are wicked and culture is cursing themselves under their own sin. It is challenging to see the Light sometimes or share our faith who would sneer mock and rebel but we must stand and fight for those souls not with weapons but with truth, love and the power of the Spirit.

Well now back to the story. In order to figure out what was going on I demanded for that thing to expose itself. The next thing I knew this old lady with grey hair in a bun came down the hall. Someone else might have said oh it's a ghost! Fortunately, I knew better. That is why we must be equipped with scripture when we are having experiences. Men have been very deceived by experiences because they did know the scripture. I said in a loud authoritative voice " in Jesus Name expose yourself"! I said with all the authority and force I could muster.

Immediately it seems as if this old lady broke into a few dozen smaller demons without much form except to say they were dark and had no light or color to them. Now they were scattered. My dad, Rev. Gary Hess, and I went through every room with anointing oil and bleeding the blood till we went to the last room. They had all gathered. There was nowhere else in the house to go.

Demons always seem to like to fight where they stay but they could not. I felt them physically try to push back. It only on rare occasions I have felt a physical manifestation but it has happened. We both commanded them to go, and eventually, they left. We have authority by the Greater One, but if you think the Enemy wont fight bac, you have another thing coming. But when we submit to God and resist the Enemy, at the end of the day he must flee and as one translation puts it "as in terror" James 4:7

When I went with my good friend J. Pollard to India in 2007, as soon as we flew over Mumbai I felt this thick darkness and strong activity of demons. This was mostly a result of idol worship and Im sure other sin that opens the door for the god of this world and his minions. Isaiah 60 describes this as gross darkness. Now in 2023 I feel even in America and other nations around the world that same kind of gross darkness if not more. Beloved, we as the ekklesia, the spiritual governing body of the Anointed in the Earth are still called to be the Light and Salt of the Earth.

We are of the Abba of lights. The time to arise and shine is more critical and essential than ever before.

So many of our social issues are connected directly to spiritual issues. Whether it be racial hatred, social division, economic collapse, government corruption, school shootings, or sexual immorality in all its forms including gender dysphoria can all have demonic influence. It usually is not just man's wickedness. I am not trying to downplay men's responsibility but I do not want to downplay the role of the Enemy either. If we could see and discern in the spirit and behold all the spirits behind so many things we might be tempted to faint.

We must remind ourselves we are not wrestling flesh and blood. Our fight is with principalities (princes of darkness) powers of the air (governors of the second heavens) spiritual wickedness in high places (influence among men with influence) dominions and might (those who roam the earth who execute the wills above them in the Earth and first heavens. It is typically these that we deal with as far as oppression among believers and potentially possession in unbelievers.

We cannot deal with these forces politically, socially or carnally. It is not by might nor by power but by the Spirit of the LORD. The ministry of seers and discerning of spirits is critical in this time to see what is really going on with the darkness and expose its deceptions. May we pray that more Seers arise and that we all shine with the light of His glory. May we proclaim and prophecy that we overcome by the blood of The Lamb and the word of *our testimony.*

Testing the Spirits

One time on my first trip with J. Pollard to India, we were asked to speak at a bible study hosted by the pastor's sister that we connected with. This pastor had dozens of small churches and pastors under him throughout Mumbai. He reminded me of what Benny

Hinn might be like if he were Indian lol. A mother had brought her two daughters who both were in their twenties. I don't remember their history. I do remember starting to teach and share the Word. Everyone seemed to be hungry. J. Pollard started praying for one of the girls. Suddenly demons started manifesting in one of them. She started screaming and sticking her tongue out. I tried to remain calm and thought I needed to explain the situation. But most there did not seem to be disturbed. They stated that this was almost normal. That was unacceptable to me for the Enemy to have such spot light and disturbance during Bible study or any time for that matter.

I started praying for her and commanding demons to come out. The first few responded more easily then some of the others. Demons like to hide when the Light shines and authority is being taken. Just because we have authority does not mean they won't fight and resist. They have been wicked and rebellious by nature since their fall. We should expect them to respond to God's command through us and His Word but many times we need to test the spirits when casting them out. I asked her to say Jesus Christ is the Son of God and He came in the flesh. John 4.

She started screaming again and sticking out her tongue. I was told that this was somehow related to Krishna. It reminded me of the scripture that talks about demons taking on the identity of gods to be worshipped. In the end we cast out seven spirits. At one point she said she felt like a man. I truly believe in my heart that the LGTQ and transgender issues/community has some level of demonic activity involved. Not to say they are all possessed but unclean spirits of lust, immorality rejection and suicide are among some of those that have given over to those thoughts lies and perceptions of their own made reality. In other words they have made their truth god when in reality a spirit is influencing to play god.

Just recently in my own city I was at the Capital praying and walking around. A homosexual couple walked past me and I saw this demon floating right with them and mocking me and cursing me as they past. I did nothing since it was not really time or place or opportunity for them to open up about that but my point is that many of these social issues are spiritual as well.

CHAPTER 6
Behold the Lamb of God

Many of the experiences I have shared thus far have been what some have deemed "open visions" I saw these things with my eyes. Yet it was not with the natural ability of my physical eyes but an extension of my spiritual eyes and supernatural work of discernment that my physical eyes could peer into the spirit realm. The scriptures speak of the third Heaven, where Paul speaks either of himself or someone else he knew, (most people believe it was himself) but in the body or out of the body, he could not tell and was taken up into the third Heaven where he witnessed unlawful things to share at that time at least.

No doubt, The LORD taught him much and many assume this is the time when Paul received much of his "Pauline revelation" that is expressed in the epistles. The third Heaven is where we think traditionally about Heaven as Paradise. There are some Jewish traditions that teach about the seven levels of Heaven, but since this is not revealed in scripture, especially in New Covenant writings, then I digress in acknowledging about those. We are now in a season, perhaps an era where the Word of the LORD is common. So many people are having visions and dreams now. There are a few "prophets" claiming to go to Heaven every other day. The last 34 thing I want to do is point a finger and say that It is a false prophet based on my own opinion or assumption. I have not had The LORD directly say so and so is false, but I will say the scripture seems to indicate visiting Heaven outside of the death experience or even dear death experience is not common. I would use caution in following someone who "visits" Heaven regularly. I have no authority to say that it can't happen but there is nothing to indicate scripturally it will happen often, either. It seems to be special.

Personally, I would not want an out-of-body experience of Heaven unless The LORD thought otherwise. I don't think I would want to come back the first time, let alone multiple times. That is why discerning spirits is so vital right now. We must know what kind of spirit we are dealing with. Even genuine prophets whose soul, emotions, mind that perhaps has been corrupted or gone through some kind of hurt can project things not of God. That is why prophets must go through wilderness training. As believers, we must all be crucified with Christ so as to be raised together with Him as Galations 2:20 proclaim.

This will help the level of pure, in-part Omniscience to flow through us by the Spirit of the Holy One. First Corinthians 13 says it this way: that we know in part and prophecy in part. Jesus Christ, according to

Revelations, is the Spirit of Prophecy. There was a time when I was not sure I wanted to see Jesus, as funny as that might seem. Before going to Rhema and not understanding my experiences, I only knew that Jesus had said blessed are you who have not seen and still believe. Well, I did 35 not want to miss out on a blessing but I finally realized seeing Jesus is the ultimate blessing. But If you have never seen anything or ever do, just remember to call yourself blessed because you still believe and great is your reward, good and faithful servant.

The first time I saw The LORD Jesus Christ, I had recently moved back to Kentucky but was visiting a friend in Tulsa, OK. He was working at World Outreach Church with Pastor Mark and Janet Brazee.

The revelation song had just come out and the worship team was singing this song. It was the first time I had heard it. They were doing a healing rally and expectation was in the air. During the song, my eyes were opened to hundreds of angels who were also worshiping and dancing in the air throughout the relatively large auditorium. The ceiling had to be at least a hundred feet, although I cannot confirm any dimensions of the church.

The angels started to gather together to form what seemed like a funnel from right above the people in the middle of the room to the ceiling and, I guess, beyond. Then I heard a voice say, "Shall I come down?' Come down, come down, the angels said. Then they all dispersed and I saw Jesus/Yeshua Elohim The Son, come down on a cloud. It is written in Deut. 33:26 and Pslams 68:5 that he rides on a cloud. Surely, the seers and prophets of old saw the Ancient of Days in visions and dreams and the Spirit gave utterance to declare what preincarnate Christ appeared to them to give a glimpse of the Glory of the Word to take on flesh. 36

So as The LORD came down to stand on the cloud hovering above the people in the middle section, I saw beams of light coming from different people who were apparently worshipping in spirit and Truth as he commanded we need to. He was absorbing this Light.

There is no human angel or creature in all creation who is worthy to receive worship and Jesus is so worthy. He gladly received His praise. It was interesting to see these beams coming from the people. After a few minutes, He said that it is My time to work. Then beams of light were coming from The LORD to different people. Pastor Brazee then proceeded to get up and he started giving words of knowledge of people being healed. I thank God for the laying on of hands, but we can also have atmospheres of faith and Glory and worship where The LORD

Himself comes and heals His people. Then my eyes were closed and shortly after that, Pastor Brazee had people come up to testify of their healing of those that he called out through Words of Knowledge. It was grand to behold. That would have happened back in 2008 or so when the Revelation song first came out.

In more recent times, 2023, in fact. I was able to witness something similar but different that blessed me as well. We were in a prayer/worship service at a relatively large church in Lexington, Ky.

I could see the LORD come down in a similar fashion after seeing angels. This time, He was right above us. I just prayed on the inside. Oh LORD, what are you going to do today? He gently said David, I AM 37 not here to work today; I AM here to enjoy the Worship of My People, but The Holy Spirit is still here. Suddenly He left and the impression I got was that He was busy. As soon as he left the worship leader of that particular service was having Words of Knowledge and he called them and laid hands on them. Goodness and power of God, especially healing and miracles, can manifest in different ways but it is the Same LORD that abounds to us His kindness that He afforded and sealed the promise of our healing through His wounds and the work of the Cross. Doubt not and believe today for you have a blessing that I may never experience for blessed are you who do believe and yet have not seen. I have seen Yeshua (Savior) on 5 occasions thus far and different forms of the Holy Spirit many times. None have seen our Heavenly Father but if we have seen Christ, even if only through the scriptures, then The Son testifies if you have seen Me you have seen the Father.

I could tell you about many other experiences that have just become a part of my life now. I have had to go through my own insecurities.Go through wilderness experiences and die to yourself. This book has been a long time coming and these experiences mean so much to me personally but now it is long overdue to share with them and testify that God is real. Many people see what is going on in the world and question what is real. I can only testify to this that God is real and that God so loved the world that He gave His only Son Jesus that whosoever would believe would not perish but have everlasting life.

Choose Life today. Choose Jesus

CHAPTER 7
Open and Closed Visions

It has been a little bit of a conundrum to figure out exactly what to share or how to end this book. I started writing this book around the end of 2020 and after the passing of my dad, Gary Hess, I had a hard time picking up the digital pen, so to speak. My experiences are continual, too. I have prayed and believed that these written down not only show a glimpse but also enough to spark inspiration and hunger to pursue and seek The LORD for yourself. To grow in gifts of the seer and prophetic if that is what your calling might be. As a believer, be encouraged that we walk by faith and not by (physical) sight. You can trust that the stories and testimonies are true and they bear witness to the testimonies of men and women of God that had theirs recorded down. I leave you with some visions I have had of late.

Most of my experiences, you could define them as open visions. More people seem to have closed visions and or dreams. I very rarely dream. I also do not usually operate in the ministry gift for the Body of tongues and interpretation. I typically would just flow in a prophecy.

But others in the Body do operate that way and also have dreams and closed visions. One is not better, simply different. The LORD is One 40 but also diverse in nature and has seen fit to provide diversity in plant life and animals along with His spiritual gifts.I am a direct kind of person. I am thankful that The LORD deals with me in this way often. Not always, but in the way of His gifts, He has been gracious. So, to those who dream, seek The LORD in the interpretation if necessary. Ask and it shall be given. Seek and you will find.

Lately, The LORD has been giving me more visions. This is slightly different than just discerning spirits as the vision is mainly in your minds/hearts eye. Recently, I had such a vision where I was praying in the middle of the night and dawn was near as I was praying in the Spirit and seeking The LORD on some things. In my mind's eye, it was as if having a waking dream. I saw this picture before me: a woman in a tattered wedding dress. She was sitting on the floor.

Her hair was black and frazzled. She was barefoot. The dress was torn in some spots and the bottom was blacked as if dragged through mud. She was crying into her knees, head covered. I never really saw her face.

Then Jesus approached her. He said get up, take off your dress, for I have a new one for you. Oh LORD, she said I am filthy, unclean and full of shame. You should not see me like this. Jesus said all the same, get up. The hour draws near and we must get you ready. She took off her tattered dress and you could see dirt and soot all over her. I knew she was naked but did not see her full nakedness. Then Jesus helped her 41 into a basin. It was not a modern bathtub but more like an old basin used back in the day to wash. He took pitchers and poured hot steaming water all over her. He washed her gently. He combed her hair. Afterward, He put on her a robe that initially looked red, dripping with blood as she was dripping from being wet. When she dried, the robe turned white.

He then called her into a room with a wardrobe that had a mirror for a door. She hesitated going up as she was still shy and even a little embarrassed to look at herself. Jesus said to look and open. She looked and saw that her countenance had changed. She opened the door and the most beautiful wedding gown was in there. At first, it seemed like it was sparkling with thousands of diamonds but looking closer, I knew now it was the precious stones of the New Jerusalem and precious stones that the high priests wore for the ephod. These, though just sparkles in the Light of Jesus, giving a subtle yet powerful rainbow effect. He said to her, it's time to get dressed. It's time to get ready. Our marriage supper is almost ready!

What a wonderful picture and representation of Jesus cleansing His people. This did not literally take place but the symbolism of the vision are very real of what The LORD is doing and preparing for us, His Bride. Much of what we see in Revelation and other places in scripture are visions that people had that symbolize truths in the spirit realm.

Interpreting such dreams and visions are necessary to comprehend what The LORD is trying to convey to us. We should avoid trying to give our own spin on it, especially in the flesh for the carnal mind cannot comprehend the things of God. We need to be transformed by the renewing of our minds to know the will of God, according to Romans 12. I could go on and on, but I believe I will leave you hear. I pray that I have inspired you and added wood to the fire and hunger to seek The LORD in deeper ways. May the Scripture and the Spirit of the Holy One by your Teacher and guide you into all Truth. Shalom and Shalom.

Now to Him who is able to (carry out His purpose and)do superabundantly more than all that we dare ask or think (infinitely beyond our greatest prayers, hopes or dreams), according to His power that is at work within us, to Him be glory in the church and in Christ Jesus throughout all generations forever and ever. Amen.

Eph. 3:20 Amp.

Seeing in the Spirit is a series of testimonies that David has experienced throughout his life. The Scriptures are the final authority when it comes to spiritual experience but it is written we overcome by the Blood of the Lamb and the word of our testimony. Our testimonies are powerful and this is God's story through David. May it minister to you, inspire you and maybe even give you courage to share your own testimony as we all want to go deeper into the realms of the Spirit with the Word of God as our Guide.

Blessings from David Hess Ministries and the entire Hess Family.

ABOUT THE AUTHOR:

David Hess is the President of David Hess Ministries aka Circle of Love Ministries. A graduate of Rhema Bible College with an associate's degree from ORU. He has been in some form of ministry since a teenager. Including youth leader, youth pastor and associate pastor. He has done short term missions trips to Eastern Europe, Africa, Australia, India and Israel. He has been called to be a prophet to the nations and a Sent One to Israel. There is also the call to cover the seven state region of the Ohio Valley in the US.

He is a Seer and has seen in the spirit realm since he was seven.

Having a deep desire to see the Body of Christ be equipped to its full potential in Christ. He preaches with passion along with a spirit of revival and revelation.